M.R. James

for the Curious

Adaptation and activities by **Eleanor Donaldson**

Illustrated by **Franco Rivolli**

Series editor: Robert Hill
Editor: Chiara Gabutti
Design and art direction: Nadia Maestri
Computer graphics: Carlo Cibrario-Sent, Simona Corniola
Picture research: Alice Graziotin

First edition: January 2015

Picture credits : Shutterstock; IstockPhoto, DreamsTime; Thinkstock;
Hulton Archive/Getty Images: 4; © Radius Images/Marka: 49;
© Benelux/Corbis: 50; © VIDEA/WebPhoto: 78.

We would be happy to receive your comments and suggestions, and
give you any other information concerning our material.
info@blackcat-cideb.com
blackcat-cideb.com

Member of CISQ Federation

RINA
ISO 9001:2008
Certified Quality System

The design, production and distribution of educational materials
for the Black Cat brand are managed in compliance with the rules of
Quality Management System which fulfils the requirements of the
standard ISO 9001 (Rina Cert. No. 24298/02/S - IQNet Reg. No. IT-80096)

Printed in Italy by Litoprint, Genoa

The text is recorded in full.

These symbols indicate the beginning and end of the passages linked to the listening activities.

About the Author

Montague Rhodes James was born in Kent in the South-East of England in 1862. M. R. James (sometimes called Monty) also lived in Suffolk. His father was a minister[1] there. The beaches and villages of this area are in many of his stories. He was interested in churches and history from the time he was a child.

He went to Eton, a well-known private school in England. Then he went to Cambridge and studied the Classics (Greek and Latin). He stayed at Cambridge to teach and study. His subject was Medieval studies and he wrote books on Medieval history, literature and theology.[2]

1. **minister** : a type of priest in some religions. (A minister can be married.)
2. **theology** : the study of religion/belief.

M. R. James was Provost at Cambridge University.

In 1886, he became the Director [3] of the University museum, the Fitzwilliam Museum. In 1905 Montague Rhodes James became the Provost [4] of Kings College at Cambridge University. He was also the Vice-Chancellor [5] of Cambridge University from 1913-1915. Later he was the Provost at Eton until he died in 1936.

Montague Rhodes James wrote his first ghost stories in magazines. He used the name M.R. James. The stories were very popular and he wrote four books of short stories in the next twenty years: *Ghost Stories of an Antiquary* (1904); *More Ghost Stories of an Antiquary* (1911); *A Thin Ghost and Others* (1919); *A Warning to the Curious and Other Ghost Stories* (1925).

3. **Director** : a manager.
4. **Provost** : head of a college or school (headmaster).
5. **Vice-Chancellor** : head of the University.

To many people, M. R. James is best-known for his ghost stories. He is often called the 'father' of the modern ghost story. The stories are about real places and real people. The main character often finds an object. The person sees a ghost or strange things happen because of this object. M. R. James gives us a warning. [6] The reader thinks: could this happen to me?

M. R. James wrote his stories for his friends and his pupils. He read them sitting next to a fire at Christmas or on dark nights. The tradition of telling these stories at Christmas continues today. There are television series of M. R. James' ghost stories and it is also possible to listen to them on the radio and on websites.

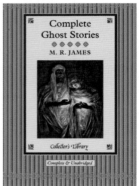

1 **Comprehension check**
Complete the sentences with information from the text.

1 Montague Rhodes was born in Kent in ....

2 Montague Rhodes studied and taught at the University of ....

4 From 1904 to 1925 M. R. James wrote .... books of short stories.

5 Montague Rhodes wrote stories for his .... and his ....

6. **warning** : something that tells you something bad could happen.

"Whistle and I'll Come to You, My Lad"

Before you read

1 **Find the words**

Look at the photographs and tick (✓) the words in the box you can see. Then look at the pictures on pages 7 and 9. Which other words can you find?

coast	nets	boat	fisherman	sand	beach	rocks	ruins
	castle	golf course	golf club	sea	stone	anchor	

2 **Adjectives**

Complete the sentences below (1-6) with an adjective (A-F).

A	curious	C	loud	E	shy
B	intelligent	D	tidy	F	well-dressed

1 ☐ She doesn't like talking to people. She is ....
2 ☐ He knows a lot of things. He is very ....
3 ☐ She likes nice clothes. She is always ....
4 ☐ He always puts everything in the right place. He is ...
5 ☐ She is interested and asks a lot of questions. She is ....
6 ☐ He is always shouting. I think he is too ....

3 **Vocabulary**

Read the title of the story on page 7. What do you think the word 'lad' means?

A ☐ a boy or young man
B ☐ a girl or young woman
C ☐ an old man or woman

The Church

It was almost Christmas and the end of the year for the students of St James College. Professor Parkins was sitting in the staff room [1] with a young lecturer in Archaeology, [2] called Mr Disney. Mr Disney was a curious young man. He always asked a lot of questions. Professor Parkins was intelligent and shy. He was well-dressed and tidy. He preferred his books to the company of other people.

'Are you going anywhere for the holidays?' the young man asked the Professor.

'I'm going to play golf,' the professor replied.

---

1. **staff room** : a room people can go when they are not working, for example, at lunch.
2. **Archaeology** : the study of history by looking at objects or buildings.

PART ONE

'Where are you going?' asked Mr Disney. 'There are some very nice places to play golf on the coast but it's quite[3] cold at this time of year.'

'I'm going to Burnstow,' said the professor. 'It's on the East coast.'

'You should visit the ruins of the old church of the Knights Templar,' began Mr Disney. 'The ruins are at the north end of the beach, near the Globe Inn. At certain times of day the sea almost covers the beach so you can't always see the church. It's a round church.' Mr Disney explained that the Knights Templar often built round churches.

'There are a lot of stories about the Knights Templar,'[4] he said. 'Of course, not all of them are true!' The professor smiled. He knew Mr Disney believed in lots of strange stories.

'I'll write to you,' he said. 'I'll tell you if I see anything interesting. I'm staying at the Globe Inn.[5] Not many guest houses are open during the winter, but the Globe Inn always stays open. I have a twin room. I don't need two beds, but I asked for a large room so I can take my books.'

'If you have another bed, then maybe I can come. I was thinking of going to visit the place myself,' said his friend.

'That's very kind,' said the professor. 'But I'd prefer to go alone. I have a lot of work to do.'

'I understand, professor. Of course, you must do your work. But remember — there are a lot of stories about ghosts in that part of the coast and it can be very lonely at this time of year!' He laughed. The professor did not think this was funny.

'I am a scientist,' he said. 'I don't believe in ghosts.'

---

3. **quite** : not a little or a lot.
4. **Knights Templar** : a religious group of knights. (See page 30.)
5. **inn** : a small hotel.

The next day professor Parkins arrived at the inn. He was very pleased with his room. It had a large desk and there was enough space for all his books. It had a window with three sides. There were beautiful views[6] from the window. The sea was only a few hundred metres from his room. The long beach continued for miles in both directions. He could see anchors, nets and the colourful boats of the fishermen. Every few metres there were low walls made of wood to stop the sea from reaching[7] the houses. In the distance, next to some small hills of grass, he could see the golf course.

There were not many guests in the Globe Inn, but the professor soon found another person interested in his favourite hobby. He was an old colonel with a big moustache and red cheeks. He knew a lot about some subjects and very little about others. He always spoke in the same loud voice. The colonel said that he was staying alone and that he was happy to play golf with the professor.

Professor Parkins spent the next day with the colonel. He was so fixed on their game of golf that it was soon late in the afternoon. They stopped for a rest.

'I should return to the hotel,' said the colonel. 'Are you coming, professor? Dinner is at six.'

'I'd like to take a walk along the beach first,' professor Parkins replied. 'I'll see you at dinner.'

There was no-one else on the beach. The professor enjoyed the silence. A cold wind blew[8] from the North. It was difficult to walk against the wind. Suddenly, the professor's foot hit a stone and he fell over between the sand and the tall grass. He stood up and looked around. In front of him he could see some old ruins.

6. **views** : the things you can see from a place.
7. **reaching** : arriving at.
8. **blew** : (past tense) to move and make air.

First, he walked around the ruins. Then he took a few steps back. The stones were in the form of a circle. He remembered Mr Disney's story about the Knights Templar and the round churches. In one corner, there was a large, high stone. It looked like the altar[9] of a church. In the centre of the altar, he saw a stone cabinet[10] filled with earth.[11] He took a small knife from his pocket and started to remove the earth inside it.

It was late now and the sun was low in the sky. The professor wanted to see inside the cabinet so he lit a match. He was unhappy to find the cabinet was empty. He lit another match. For a moment, he saw something. Then the wind blew out the match. He put his hand inside the cabinet and he found a small object. It was long and made of metal. He took it and put it in his pocket.

'I'll look at it later,' he thought, and he started walking towards the hotel.

Once or twice he looked back towards the ruins. In the distance, he saw a tall black figure[12] in the pale[13] evening light. A man was walking along the beach in the same direction. Every time he looked back, the man was behind him. At first the figure was far from him but then he seemed to come closer. It seemed like he was trying to reach the professor. Did he know him? He thought for a moment of waiting for him but he decided this was not a good idea. It was now dark. The professor was alone and the man was a stranger.[14]

'He must be going the same way,' he said to himself. He walked quickly towards the hotel. Then he started to run.

9. **altar** : a table used for religious ceremonies.
10. **cabinet** : a type of cupboard to keep things in.
11. **earth** : the ground is made of this; plants can grow in it.
12. **figure** : the shape of a person you cannot see very well.
13. **pale** : no colour.
14. **stranger** : someone a person has never met before.

The text and **beyond**

1 KEY **Comprehension check**

For each question choose the correct answer — A, B or C.

1 Where was the professor going to stay?

   A ☐ At a golf course on the west coast.

   B ☐ At an inn in the countryside.

   C ☐ In a seaside town called Burnstow.

2 What did Mr Disney say the professor should see?

   A ☐ The church of the Knights Templar.

   B ☐ The golf course near the ruins.

   C ☐ The view from the bedrooms in the Globe Inn.

3 What type of room did the professor have?

   A ☐ A single room.

   B ☐ A twin room.

   C ☐ A double room.

4 What did the professor find after his game of golf?

   A ☐ The ruins of a castle in the sand.

   B ☐ Another golf course.

   C ☐ The ruins of an old church.

5 What did the professor find in the cabinet?

   A ☐ A long metal object.

   B ☐ A small knife.

   C ☐ An altar filled with earth.

6 Why did the professor begin to run?

   A ☐ He saw a man from the hotel he didn't like.

   B ☐ He was late to meet the colonel for dinner.

   C ☐ Maybe he was scared of the stranger.

2 Vocabulary – Rooms

A Complete the sentences 1-4 with a word from the word box.

wardrobe	washbasin	armchair	forks

1 bath, toilet, towel, ...
2 bed, sheet, blanket, ...
3 sofa, television, rug, ...
4 table, chairs, knives, ...

B In which room (A-D) can you find the objects in each group?

A ☐ living room
B ☐ bedroom
C ☐ dining room
D ☐ bathroom

3 Describing a room

Use the example to describe a room you know.

Example: In the top right corner there are some bookshelves. In the centre of the room there is a table.

Work with a partner:

A describes a room to B.

B draws the room.

A looks at the picture of B. Does it look like the room A described?

'I'm going to play golf'

We use *going to + verb* to talk about something we plan to do in the future. This is something we know will happen or that we will do. We can also use the present continuous if we have a fixed arrangement, for example *'I am playing golf with the colonel tomorrow.'*

4 Verbs – Sport

Use *going to + go* or *going to + play* to make sentences using the words
A-H. You can use *I, he, she, we* or *they*. *Example: I am going to play tennis.*

A tennis
B rock climbing
C football
D jogging

E swimming
F cycling
G snowboarding
H rugby

5 Hobbies and sports

Answer the questions below about your hobbies and the sports you
like to watch and play.

1   Do you have a hobby? What is it?
2   What sports do you like to watch/play?
3   When do you do your hobbies? When do you play sport?

Before you read

1 Odd one out

A   Find the odd one out.

   1   whistle, flute, trumpet, club
   2   sound, note, wind, song
   3   key, guitar, piano, violin

B   What best connects the other words in each group 1-3?

   A ☐ weather   **B** ☐ music   **C** ☐ sport

2 Sounds

Listen to the sounds. Number them in the order you hear them.

☐ wind   ☐ guitar   ☐ golf   ☐ sea   ☐ whistle   ☐ rain

A Sleepless[1] Night

rofessor Parkins changed his clothes and went to dinner. The colonel asked him about his walk.

'The staff at the hotel were worried about you. It gets dark very early at this time of year,' he added.

The professor decided not to say anything about the man on the beach. He was tired after his long walk and he decided to go to bed early. On the way to his room, one of the waiters stopped him.

'Something fell out of your coat pocket, sir,' he said. 'The maid[2] put it in your room.'

---

1. **sleepless** : without sleep.
2. **maid** : a woman who cleans/makes the bed, etc. in a hotel.

PART **TWO**

'Thank you,' said professor Parkins. He returned quickly to his bedroom.

He picked up the object on the desk and looked at it carefully. There was a lot of sand in it. The professor put the sand on some paper and threw it out of the window. He stopped for a moment and looked out. In the distance, he saw a man on the beach.

'It's a cold night to be outside!' he said to himself. He shut the window and returned to the object. It had some small holes in it. It looked like a whistle. In fact, it was a whistle. There was some writing on it in Latin: "Quis est iste qui venit". He knew a little Latin so he translated [3] the words.

'*Who is coming?*'

'An interesting question. What does it mean? "*Who is coming?*"' he repeated. 'I have the whistle... Maybe I should use the whistle and then I'll see!'

He blew the whistle once. He was surprised at the sound. The sound continued for a long time. It was a soft note, like music. Sometimes it was high and sometimes it was low. For a moment, in front of his eyes, he saw a person. It looked like the man on the beach, but he could not see his face.

Suddenly, the wind began to blow hard. The windows blew open. The air went quickly through the windows and blew out the candle on the desk. He tried to close the windows but the wind was too strong! He thought the glass was going to break. He pushed hard against the windows. For a moment, he imagined the wind was a stranger trying to enter his room. Finaly he shut them. But the windows continued to shake.

'It's incredible how the wind can change so quickly!' he thought

---

3. **translated** : changed words into a different language.

as he listened to the wind. 'The weather is a very interesting thing. I work with facts, not fiction. But a man could imagine things on a night like this.' For many hours the wind continued its lonely cry and he couldn't sleep. Every time he closed his eyes he saw the same thing. This was what he saw:

It was a winter's evening and the clouds in the sky were grey. There was a man in black clothes on the beach. The man was weak[4] and tired. He looked very frightened. He was trying to escape from someone or something. The man climbed over the sea walls. Sometimes he looked behind him. Then he saw a figure. At first it looked like a bird. Then it looked like a man in a white cloak.[5] The figure in the white cloak moved quickly towards the man. The man hid behind one of the walls. The figure came closer. It held its arms open. Its long cloak was like wings. It moved towards the man again. This time, the professor opened his eyes. It was like a film, but he did not want to see the end.

He sat up in bed and read one of his books. He heard the sound of something moving near the second bed. 'Rats,' he thought. 'Rats like old buildings like this.'

He fell asleep some hours later. The candle was still burning.

The following morning, there was a knock[6] at the door. It was the maid.

'I've come to make the bed, sir,' she said. 'Can I come in?'

The professor saw it was late in the morning. He put on his dressing gown.

---

4.   **weak** : not strong.
5.   **cloak** : a type of coat without a place for arms. It ties at the neck.
6.   **knock** : a noise made by hitting something.

'Would you like another blanket?'

'Yes, please,' he said. 'It was quite cold last night. The wind was bad as well.'

'Maybe someone was whistling,' she said.

'What a strange idea!' said professor Parkins. 'Why do you say that?'

'Oh, it's something people say in the village: "The wind comes when someone is whistling". It's an old legend. I don't know where it comes from.'

'Really?' he said, trying not to sound too interested. 'Now — the blanket. I'll take it if you want.'

'No, sir. It's no trouble. Where do you want me to put it?'

'On my bed,' he said, a little surprised by the question.

'Which one, sir?' she asked. 'It looks like there was someone in both beds.'

'I don't know what you mean,' the professor replied.

He looked at the second bed. One of the sheets was on the floor and the other sheet was very creased. [7] The maid was right. It looked like two people were staying in the room.

'Perhaps the sheet fell on the floor in the night,' he said. 'Maybe, it was the wind. I'm sorry to give you more work.'

The maid started to make the other bed. The professor left the room a little red in the face.

'Very strange,' he said to himself. 'Very strange...'

---

7. **creased** : lined from being touched.

The text and **beyond**

1 **Find the missing words**

Read the questions (1-6). Complete the missing words in the answers (A-F). The first letter is already there.

1   What fell out of the professor's pocket?

    An object he found at the r _ _ _ _ . It was a w _ _ _ _ _ _ .

2   What happened when the professor blew the whistle?

    The w _ _ _ started to b _ _ _ hard.

3   Who did the professor see when he closed his eyes?

    A man followed by another man in a w _ _ _'_ c _ _ _ _ .

4   What did he think made the noise under the other bed?

    He thought there were r _ _ _ in the room.

5   Why did the maid come to the room?

    To make the b _ _ .

6   Why did the maid think two people were staying in the room?

    The s _ _ _ _ _ on both beds were c _ _ _ _ _ _ _ .

2 **Puzzle**

Complete the puzzle with the missing words from exercise 1 to see the word in red. Words can go across or down.

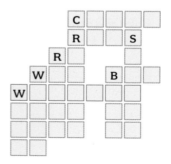

3 **Fact or fiction?**

The professor is a scientist. He believes in fact not fiction. Can you guess if the sentences 1-6 are Fact or Fiction?

		Fact	Fiction
1	One country separates Finland and North Korea.	☐	☐
2	Peanuts are not nuts.	☐	☐
3	The moon is made of cheese.	☐	☐
4	Dragons once lived in parts of Wales.	☐	☐
5	Some clouds are the same weight as several blue whales.	☐	☐
6	A monkey was once sent to the centre of the earth.	☐	☐

4 **Listening – Housekeeping**

Listen to someone talking to a maid. Tick the jobs you hear.

1 ☐ Put clean towels in the bathroom.
2 ☐ Check the lamp is working.
3 ☐ Open the window.
4 ☐ Put shower gel in the shower.
5 ☐ Make the bed.
6 ☐ Put flowers in the room.

5 **Conversations**

Complete the conversations and practice them. (You can use your own words.)

1 These sheets are creased. Can I have new ones?
Of .... I'll .... them now.

2 Hello, I have a reservation.
What's your ....?

3 What would you like for dinner?
I'd .... some/the ....

Before you read

1 Superstitions

A Find the word 'superstition' in a dictionary. Then match the descriptions A-F to a picture (1-6).

  a walking under a ladder
  b breaking a mirror
  c four leafed clover (a type of plant)
  d fingers crossed
  e Friday the thirteenth
  f touch wood

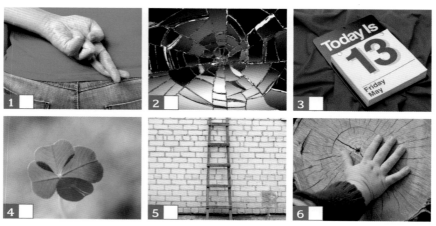

B Answer the questions.

  1 Do the things in exercise 1A bring good or bad luck?
  2 Are there any superstitions in your country?

2 Reading pictures
Look at the picture on page 29 and answer the questions.

  1 Where is the professor?
  2 What is happening in the picture?
  3 What do you think will happen next?

The Empty Bed

The two men were playing their second game of golf. The weather was much better and the light wind was pleasant.

'Incredible wind we had last night!' the colonel began.

'The maid seemed to have some silly [1] idea about someone whistling for the wind!' the professor said.

'It could be true,' said the colonel. 'The villagers know things we don't.'

'I don't believe in these old stories,' said the professor. 'As an example, I found a whistle on the beach last night. I tried to whistle with it. A few moments later, the wind blew very hard. It shook the windows. A person could say that I brought the wind. But I know that

---

1. **silly** : stupid and funny.

the wind doesn't come because you whistle for it. The wind is part of the changes in the weather. It is science, not some strange event.' The colonel was suddenly interested. He put down his golf clubs.

'This whistle... ,' said the colonel. 'Where did you find it?'

'I found it at the old church of the Knights Templar. Why?' asked the professor.

'You found it at the ruins!' He shook his head. 'I don't think you should trust[2] it. It's not a good idea to take something from a religious place. You must know the legends. Have you never heard the stories about the Knights Templar? For many years, I was in the army in India...' he began.

Professor Parkins knew the colonel was going to tell a long story, so he picked up his golf clubs again. On their way around the golf course the colonel told him of his adventures. He talked of the superstitions of the villages and how one night he saw a ghost himself.

The professor was going to tell him his ideas about ghosts, but he was interrupted[3] by a young boy who came running towards the two men. He was crying.

'What the matter, boy?' asked the colonel. 'Are you lost?'

'There's a man at the window!' he cried.

'Which window?' asked the colonel.

'That window! There it was!' he said. He pointed to the hotel and to the window with three sides. It was Professor Parkins's room.

'It?' asked the professor. 'You said you saw a man.'

'It was like a man... but it wasn't a man. I didn't like the face.' The boy started to cry again.

'It was probably a silly joke,' said the colonel. 'Don't cry. Here,

2. **trust** : believe it is good and will not hurt someone.
3. **interrupted** : to stop someone from speaking.

take some money. There's a café that sells ice-cream near the hotel. You'll soon feel better.'

Professor Parkins turned to the colonel. 'I'd like to go back to the hotel,' he said. 'We can finish our game tomorrow.'

Professor Parkins went to his room. The door was locked. Everything inside the room was the same. But there was one small difference — the empty bed was not made.

'But I saw the maid making the bed this morning!' He shook his head and went to find the maid.

'Does anyone have the key to my room?' he asked.

'The manager keeps all they keys. I gave the key to him this morning,' she said. Professor Parkins went to see the manager. He told him the story about the child.

'Was anything missing?' the manager asked.

He wanted to tell him about the bed but then he didn't want the maid to be in trouble.

'No, everything's fine. Perhaps it was the child imagining things or maybe it was a different room.' He left quickly. He was angry with himself. There must be a reason [4] but he didn't know the answer.

Later that night, the professor studied the whistle again. He thought of the colonel's words: 'I don't trust it! You should throw it in the sea!' He put it back on the desk. He went to the door and closed it with the key. Then he went to the windows. They were closed, too. He saw for the first time that there were no curtains in his room. The light of the full moon shone through the windows and into the room. The professor didn't want another sleepless night, so he took the blanket from the second bed and made a curtain. He fell asleep quickly.

4. **reason** : the facts about why something is happening.

A few hours later he woke up when the curtain fell to the ground and made a noise. Then he heard another loud noise. The noise was coming from the empty bed. The bed was shaking. There, sitting in the other bed, was a white figure. The figure slowly got out of bed and moved towards the professor. The figure's face was full of lines like the creased sheets. It had no eyes but it had a large, open mouth.

Professor Parkins jumped up. He tried to go to the door, but he couldn't reach the key. The figure now stood between the bed and the door. The professor moved quickly towards the window. The figure continued to follow him with its long arms held out. Its fingers almost touched his face. The professor put one leg out of the window. He looked down. Could he jump? The figure came closer. At that moment he felt a cold face push against his neck. He cried out in terror.

The colonel arrived at that moment. Professor Parkins climbed back into the room and fainted. [5] On the floor, next to the professor, were the bed sheets but there was no one there. The colonel stayed for the rest of the night and the professor sat in an armchair as white as the sheets on the floor.

The next day the colonel spoke to the hotel manager. He said he was sorry the other guests woke up to loud noises. The professor sometimes had bad dreams.

Professor Parkins still doesn't believe in ghosts but he is less certain about things now. The professor did not return the whistle; he threw it into the sea as far away as he could. He told Mr Disney there was nothing interesting to see at the ruins. He never returned to Burnstow or to the church of the Knights Templar.

---

5. **fainted** : to be unconscious (not awake) for a short time.

The text and **beyond**

1 **True or false**

Are the sentences true (T) of false (F)?

		T	F
1	The colonel thinks all superstitions are silly.	☐	☐
2	The boy points to the professor's room.	☐	☐
3	The professor's room was not locked.	☐	☐
4	The figure in white moves towards the professor.	☐	☐
5	The professor doesn't jump from the window.	☐	☐
6	The professor now believes in ghosts.	☐	☐

CULTURE SPOT

The History of the Knights Templar

The Knights Templar were a group of religious knights. They fought in many battles but they were also like monks. They had to follow the beliefs of their Order.

The Order began in the city of Jerusalem (now in Israel) in 1118 A.D. at the time of the first Crusade. The Crusades were religious wars over many hundreds of years in an area called the Holy Land (Israel and Palestine). The knights wanted to protect pilgrims going to the Holy Land. The Knights Templar started to wear white cloaks, called mantles, with a red cross on them.

The Knights Templar soon had many thousands of knights and the Order became rich and powerful. The Templars built churches on the land, called preceptories, and they buried their dead there.

After almost two hundred years, the Templars started to lose their power and their battles. The Order had to close. In 1312, the Pope gave the Templar's possessions to another order. Many of the knights went to other countries. They continued to meet in secret, or became part of other orders.

Today there is a modern Order of the Knights Templar. They have a website and they have preceptories. They are not rich or powerful, but the many stories and legends of the Order of the Knights Templar continue to this day.

Answer the questions about the text.

1 Who were the Knights Templar?

2 Where did the Order begin?

3 Who did the knights want to protect?

4 What did the knights wear?

5 When did the Order close?

6 Is there an Order of the Knights Templar today?

2 Characters

Choose a character. Write three things you know from the story and three things using your imagination. Test another student. Can they remember the facts from the story?

Example: *The professor doesn't believe in ghosts. He always has tea at four o'clock.*

3 Writing your own ghost story

Here are some adjectives you can find in ghost stories. Use your imagination to make sentences using the nouns (A-G). For example: *'There was a haunted house'.*

lonely	cold	dark	haunted	pale	terrible	old

A house

B church

C wood

D beach

E figure

F smell

G tree

Now complete the story with your own words. Repeat the last words in the first line, as in the example.

> *In a spooky village there was a dark wood. Near the dark wood there was an old house.*
>
> *In/near/next to/outside the old house there was ...*

The Knights Templar:
Legends and Hidden Treasure

At the time of the Crusades, the knights protected the Temple of King Solomon. The legend says they took some treasure with them when they left. Some people believe they also found a secret.

One possibility is Rosslyn Chapel in Scotland. There are tales that the knights went to Scotland. They stayed at a place called Rosslyn and hid their treasure in the chapel. There are special symbols in the chapel. Many people believe the Templars left these symbols. They think they left a secret message about the place where the 'Holy Grail' lies. In legend, it is said the person who drinks from the Holy Grail will live forever.

There are also stories of hidden treasure in France and Spain. The Templars hid their money there from the King of France.

There are many books and films about the Templars. Some of these stories are true but most are fiction. The most famous of these books in modern times is the *Da Vinci Code* by Dan Brown. The Da Vinci Code is also a film. In the Da Vinci Code, the treasure is not an object. It is some important information. Maybe we will never know the true secrets of the Templars or their treasure.

The Treasure of Abbot Thomas

Before you read

1 **Find the words**

You will find the words in the word box in the story. Find their meaning. Which things/people could you find in a monastery?

abbey	courtyard	chapel	code	clue
abbot	painting (noun)		cloaks	monks
minister	cross	statue	well (noun)	

2 **What are they made of?**

Find the best match.

1 ☐ leather   **A** well
2 ☐ glass   **B** ring
3 ☐ gold   **C** window
4 ☐ marble   **D** bag

3 **Title**

Look at the picture on page 33 and at the tiltle (page 35). What is the window made of?

4 **A message**

Read the message and answer the questions.

Beware! The Treasure has a guardian.

1   What does the word 'beware' mean in this sign?
    A ☐ Don't touch!   **B** ☐ Stop!   **C** ☐ Be careful!

2   What does a guardian do?
    A ☐ protects   **B** ☐ fights   **C** ☐ stays in one place

The Stained Glass Window

How incredible to find such a rare book! I could be a rich man!' cried Mr Somerton. The antiques dealer was a small man of around fifty years old. He knew a lot about antiques. He also knew a lot about making money.

The book in front of the antiques dealer was not in English, it was in Latin. It was a guide to the Abbey of Steinfield from 1100 to 1540. The antiques dealer was looking for some important pages about a stained glass window. The window belonged to one of his customers, Lord Denby. This is the translation of those pages.

There are many stories about the Abbey of Steinfield. The best known of these tales is that one of the Abbots, Abbot Thomas, hid a large bag of gold[1] in the abbey. To this day no-one has ever found it.

1. gold :

> *A report tells us that the abbot's last words before he died were:*
> *'Only three people can help the person who looks for the gold. But I*
> *am not worried about anyone finding the gold! It is safe.'*
>
> *During the Abbot's time at the abbey, he added some interesting*
> *new parts to the chapel and the Abbot's House. There was a large*
> *stained glass window and a well made of fine Italian marble.*
> *Today, the well is in the courtyard next to the Abbot's House.*

There was a painting[2] of the window in the book. In the painting there were three figures on the right and a coat of arms[3] on the left. There was also a picture of the abbot.

'The monastery closed for the first time in the sixteenth century. Many of its treasures went to other countries,' he read. 'No-one has ever found the window but many people believe it is in England.'

Mr Somerton visited Lord Denby the next day and asked to visit his private chapel. He saw that there were three large figures on the stained glass window. Each one had beautifully painted cloaks. They held a scroll[4] in their hands. There was a sentence on each scroll. The antiques dealer wrote down the three sentences.

> *There is a place where the gold lies.*
> *No man knows the writing on their clothes.*
> *On one stone there are seven eyes.*

Mr Somerton was sure that he was looking at the same window. On the left, there was a coat of arms and a picture of a man next to it. Mr Somerton read the name below it. It was Abbot Thomas. He was very excited about his find. He carefully examined everything.

2. **painting** : a picture.
3. **coat of arms** : a symbol of identity; it is often used by important families or places.
4. **scroll** :

'"There is a place where the gold lies." The window tells of the gold hidden by the abbot, like the story in the book. "No man knows the writing on their clothes." The clue must be their cloaks,' he thought.

Mr Somerton touched the side of one of the cloaks with his pen. Some black paint remained. He pressed the pen to the glass again. This time he scratched [5] the paint. It came away easily. He turned around to see Lord Denby standing behind him.

'Good morning, Lord Denby,' he said, a little surprised. 'I'm sorry. My hands are very dirty with the dust [6] from the windows.'

'I will call someone to clean the windows at once,' Lord Denby said to him. 'Please, continue with your work.'

The antiques dealer said he was trying to find something important. He just needed to remove some of the paint around the cloaks. The paint was not part of the original window. Lord Denby's window was worth [7] a lot of money, he added. Lord Denby had an important meeting but he was happy for Mr Somerton to continue his studies of the window. A few moments later, the cleaner arrived with a hard brush. [8]

'Let me do this,' Mr Somerton told the cleaner. 'This is a very old window. I know how to clean it.' The antiques dealer immediately started to remove the paint. At first he saw a letter, then another letter... and another! There were letters all around the cloaks. First, he copied all the letters. Then he tried to make sentences. The letters meant nothing!

---

5. **scratched** : to make a long thing mark/cut.
6. **dust** : very small pieces of dirt; you see it in the air or on objects.
7. **worth** : how much someone will pay for something.
8. **brush** :

'Of course!' cried Mr Somerton. 'Why didn't I think of it before? The abbot is a very clever man! The letters are written in code. But soon I will find out his secret.'

Mr Somerton returned to his home in Parsbury. He spent many nights trying to find the answer to the code. He tried all the different types of code he knew. He tried numbers and other letters, he tried ancient languages and he tried maths. It was still impossible. He could not find the answer to the code!

Finally, he opened the book about the Abbey. He studied the picture of the window. There was something interesting about the hands of the figures. The fingers all pointed in the same direction. There was only one difference. The first figure pointed [9] with one figure, the second with two fingers and the third ...

'That's it!' he cried. 'One finger and I jump one place to the next letter - 'T'. Now, two fingers - jump two places to the next letter, that's 'E'. Three fingers — jump three places...'

The answer to the code was in front of his eyes! He started to underline each of the letters.

T̲XEV B̲NGKH T̲GH T̲R O̲YPAURSJ Z̲A̲DBM N̲XQ D̲

He was soon looking at a hidden message.

Ten thousand pieces of gold are kept in a well in the court of the Abbot's House of Steinfield. Beware! The treasure has a guardian.

Mr Somerton knew what he must do next. The possibility of finding hidden treasure was very exciting. He had to go to Steinfield.

9.   **pointed** : to use a finger (fingers) to show someone a person, an object, etc.

The text and **beyond**

1 Summary

Put the sentences in the order you read about them in the story.

A ☐ The book tells of an Abbot who hid some gold.
B ☐ Mr Somerton leaves for Steinfield.
C ☐ He removes some paint from the cloaks.
D ☐ He thinks there is a clue in the stained glass window.
E ☐ The antiques dealer makes a translation from a rare book.
F ☐ Mr Somerton goes to Lord Denby's chapel.
G ☐ The code tells him the place the abbot hid the gold.
H ☐ Under the cloaks he finds some letters.

2 Draw a coat of arms

A Look at the coat of arms on the right. What symbol does it have?

a ☐ a snake **b** ☐ a dragon **c** ☐ a horse

B Imagine you have a coat of arms. Draw your coats of arms. Explain it to another person.

Example: the symbol on my coat of arms is a fish. It also has the sea because my village is next to the sea.

3 Secret codes

A Can you remember the code in the story? How does the antiques dealer find the answer?

B Read the secret codes. Can you guess the words? (Clue — write the alphabet in a circle. There are only three numbers you need to know: 1, 2, 3)

XMR VGIK QBD Y PSYQTC KDVQ SM QFD UBKJ
RMJDMKD GP VYQBFFME BNS
QGWVPK SFB RRLMC ZLA XMR VGIK JFUC

C Write a sentence in the code. Ask another student to guess the meaning.

④ Multiple choice

Read the text and decide which answer best fit each space — A, B or C.

The monasteries in the 16th century

The early 16th century was a time **(1)** .... big changes in the religion and politics of England and other European countries.

The church at this time was very powerful. A lot of people felt it had too **(2)** .... power. It was also very rich. A man **(3)** .... Martin Luther started a new church. The people who followed the new religion, later called Protestants, preferred very simple traditions. They **(4)** .... not want gold or expensive objects in their churches. Kings, Princes and other important people, saw that they could use this change to close the monasteries and take everything **(5)** .... could. Some stole from the monasteries and the monks ran away and had to hide their possessions. In many places, the monasteries **(6)** .... ruins.

1	**A**	of	**B**	because	**C**	to
2	**A**	many	**B**	big	**C**	much
3	**A**	he	**B**	called	**C**	name
4	**A**	were	**B**	do	**C**	did
5	**A**	they	**B**	he	**C**	them
6	**A**	was	**B**	became	**C**	become

Before you read

1 **Listening**

Listen to part of the Part Two. Tick the things that the servant takes with him in his bag. If you do not know these words, find them in a dictionary.

metal	bars	a rope	a lantern	a cross
	some candles	a leather bag		a toad

2 **Smells**

Find these words. What smells worse?

A mould **B** dust **C** rotten eggs

3 **Vocabulary – Animals and other creatures**

Answer the questions.

1 Which of these has tentacles?

2 Which of these do you think makes a good guardian?

3 Look at the picture on page 42. What creature can you see?

The Guardian of the Treasure

Mr Gregory, the minister of Parsbury, was going for his morning walk when he saw the postman arrive at the gate.

'Ah, the post is early!' he said happily. The postman gave him a letter.

'It has got a foreign stamp on it,' the postman said. The letter was from the servant of his friend, Mr Somerton. This is what he read:

'Sir, the master is very sick. He won't get out of bed. He needs a friend and he asks you to help him. He will pay all your expenses.'[1] The letter gave the address of a guest house in the village of Steinfield in Germany.

You can imagine the surprise and the confusion[2] of Mr Gregory.

---

1. **expenses** : the cost of travelling, eating, etc.
2. **confusion** : not being able to understand or think easily.

His friend was in trouble. There was no time to lose. A few hours later he was on a train to Europe.

Two days later the minister arrived in Steinfield. He took a carriage [3] directly to the guest house. The servant was already waiting at the door. He took Mr Gregory to see his master.

The room was at the end of a long, dark, narrow [4] corridor. It had a small door and Mr Gregory had to lower his head to go in. The room was in almost complete darkness. The only light came from a small opening in the curtains. Mr Somerton was sitting in bed.

'Is that you my dear friend?' he cried out in the dark. 'Thank you for coming so quickly.' Mr Gregory came closer to the bed. He saw that his friend looked thin and pale. There were drops [5] of sweat [6] on his face and his hands were shaking.

'Gregory, I need you to help me,' he said. 'I can't tell you everything, but tomorrow morning there is something you must do. Brown will tell you everything you need to know. There is something you must put back. I'm afraid something terrible will happen.'

Mr Gregory did exactly what Mr Somerton asked. He went with Mr Brown to the Abbey of Steinfield and he followed his instructions. Then he returned to the guest house.

The next day, Mr Somerton said he was feeling better and they decided to return to England. On the return journey, Mr Gregory finally asked Mr Somerton about the strange events at Steinfield. His friend told him the story of the stained glass window in Lord Denby's chapel. He told him about the book and how he found the answer to the code.

'Brown and I came immediately to Steinfield,' he continued.

---

3. **carriage** : an old vehicle pulled by horses.
4. **narrow** : thin; not wide
5. **drop** :
6. **sweat** : drops of this are made when a person is hot.

¹ 'On the first day, we went to find the Abbey. The book told me everything I needed to know. Mr Somerton described the abbey, the Abbot's House and how they found the courtyard with the well made of fine Italian marble.

'I looked down to the bottom of the well. And to my surprise, each stone looked like a step. But what if it was trick? And if I stood on the wrong step? Could it open a hole in the well or could it be something worse? It didn't matter. We were well prepared. We returned that night. Brown brought a rope and some metal bars for climbing. He also had some candles and a lantern. I climbed down into the well with the rope tied around me. I looked at each step for a clue. At the forty-ninth step I reached the bottom. There was nothing there. I felt very unhappy. We couldn't travel all this way for nothing! We started to go back up the steps. At the thirty-eighth step, my boot hit the stone hard. A large piece of stone broke off. Brown was behind me now, holding the lantern. 'It's a funny cross,' he said. He was looking at the step. 'It looks like eyes.'

'That's it!' I cried. I took the lantern out of Brown's hand. Three eyes went across and four eyes went down. I remembered the words of the third scroll. "On one stone there are seven eyes." I hit the stone in the centre of the cross and the stone moved. I took the stone out of the wall and put it on the step below. I lit a candle and looked into the hole. Very slowly I put my arm into the hole until my fingers touched something. It was an old leather bag. I pulled the bag towards me....

Mr Somerton stopped. He turned to his servant and asked for a drink. Finally he was able to continue with his story.

'I was terrified. The smell of the bag was terrible. It was the

worst smell of mould[8] I have ever smelt. I felt something cold press itself against my face. It wrapped itself tightly around my body; its arms and legs were like tentacles around my neck. I couldn't breathe. I couldn't escape. I fell from the step into the well. But I still had the rope around me and Brown was able to pull me up. Now, Brown will tell you his story.'

'Well, sir,' said Brown. 'The master was looking in the hole and I was holding the lantern. I heard someone laughing like a mad man at the top of the well. I ran up the steps and I held the light to his face. He had a horrible old face — the skin hung from his bones. His mouth was open and laughing and I could see his rotten[9] yellow teeth. Just at that moment, I heard the master cry. I don't know how I had the strength to pull him up with the rope.'

'After I returned to my room that night,' said Mr Somerton in a low voice. 'He sent someone to watch me.'

'Do you mean Abbot Thomas?' Mr Gregory asked.

'I think the man Brown saw was the Abbot, but I believe the stone has a guardian. In the night I heard noises outside my door and I knew there was someone watching me because each time they came there was the the same smell of mould. I knew that the best thing to do was to return stone to its place and I needed someone I could trust. I am curious to know: did you see anything strange this morning?'

'The task was easy,' said Mr Gregory. 'Brown and I put the stone back quite quickly. The things you left were still there. I didn't sleep well the night before. I felt someone watching me, too. I had the same feeling when I put the stone back. There was a statue on the edge of the well. When we left, I looked at the statue again. It was smiling. It had the face of a very ugly toad.'

8. **mould** : something is old and has water in it.
9. **rotten** : gone bad.

The text and **beyond**

1 **Comprehension check**

Match the questions 1-6 with an answer A-F.

1 ☐ What does Mr Gregory receive?

2 ☐ Where was Mr Somerton when Mr Gregory arrived?

3 ☐ What did Mr Somerton ask Mr Gregory to do?

4 ☐ How did Mr Somerton and his servant go down the well.

5 ☐ Why did Mr Somerton scream?

6 ☐ What did Mr Gregory see before he left?

A There were some steps inside the well.

B He asked him to put something back.

C He received a letter from Mr Somerton's servant.

D He saw a statue of a very ugly toad.

E He was sitting in bed.

F He felt something wrap itself around his body.

2 **KEY** **A letter**

Complete the reply to Mr Somerton's servant from Mr Gregory. Write one word for each space.

Dear Mr Brown,

Thank you for your letter.

I was very sad (1) .... hear about the news about my friend, Mr Somerton. I (2) .... leaving for Germany after I post this letter. If I take the train this evening, I (3) .... arrive in Steinfield (4) .... Wednesday.

I'm sure (5) .... the help of his friends your master will soon be better. I look forward to seeing (6) .... soon.

Best wishes,

Mr Gregory

3 **Vocabulary – Types of transport**

Tick the types of transport that Mr Gregory uses to travel to Europe.
What other ways are there to travel?

☐ train   ☐ bicycle   ☐ aeroplane

☐ carriage   ☐ taxi   ☐ boat

4 **Travel**

Answer the questions about travel.

1   How do you travel to school/work?

2   How do you prefer to travel?

3   Is it faster to travel by train or by plane?

5 **Writing instructions**

Mr Somerton gives Mr Gregory some instructions. Complete the
instructions with a verb or *don't* + a verb. Add some more of your own.

> put   open   take   go   look

.... *for the courtyard.* .... *too near the well!*
.... *the stone back carefully!* .... *the bag we left near*
the well!
.... *your door at night!*

6 **Spooky Corner**

You are going to look for secret treasure at night. Decide with another
student what you should take with you. Describe the things you took.
For example:

{ *We took a torch and some matches.* }

Ghost Stories

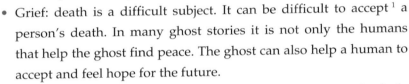

Why do people tell ghost stories?

Many countries around the world have tales of spirits and ghosts. Here are some of the reasons people tell ghost stories.

- A warning to others: some ghost stories are tales about what will happen if someone doesn't do things correctly. For example, not burying a dead body correctly.
- Grief: death is a difficult subject. It can be difficult to accept [1] a person's death. In many ghost stories it is not only the humans that help the ghost find peace. The ghost can also help a human to accept and feel hope for the future.
- To entertain: it is exciting to listen to a good ghost story, in the dark, next to a fire. We enjoy being frightened.

A History of Ghost Stories

Before the 1800s, people often told ghost stories in villages or religious believers talked of spirits. Many people believed ghosts were the spirits of the dead and they prayed for the spirits so they could go to heaven. These stories were not scary.

In the late 1700s and early 1800s, a new type of story became popular. These were called 'Gothic Horror'. These stories were not real. The events happened in castles, old ruins, and dark, cold places. *The Castle of Otranto*, by Horace Walpole is one of the first books of this type, but

---

1. **accept** : understand something is true.

there are many other famous books like *Frankenstein* by Mary Shelley and *Dracula* by Bram Stoker.

The ghost stories we know today began later in the 19th century. In these stories, the ghosts are often bad spirits. Sometimes the ghosts teach people how to live better lives. In *A Christmas Carol* by Charles Dickens, three ghosts show a man what will happen if he doesn't change. The next day he changes the way he behaves.

Ghost stories and horror stories became popular with American writers. Some well-known writers are Edgar Allan Po and Edith Wharton. These writers also wrote short stories. Some ghost stories are funny and entertaining. In the *Canterville Ghost* by Oscar Wilde, for example, the family tell the ghost to go away and stop making trouble. In the end, a child is able to help the ghost to find peace.

Another famous ghost story of this time is *The Turn of the Screw* by Henry James. In *The Turn of the Screw,* the reader doesn't know if there is really a ghost. It could be the imagination of the main character. Or maybe it is the imagination of the reader!

M. R. James had many good examples of ghost stories to use, but his stories are special. His stories are not horror stories. The reader must imagine the ghost or feel it is near. Modern ghost stories often follow this example. We should feel scared but not terrified. M. R. James called this feeling a 'pleasing terror.'

Comprehension check

4 **Which of these words best describe a ghost story?**

| entertaining | frightening | exciting | scary |
| horrible | terrifying | funny | |

The Tractate Middoth

Before you read

1 **KEY** **Vocabulary – In the library**
Read the descriptions of people, objects and things you do in a library.
What is the word for each one? The first letter is already there.

1   Information on paper or in a computer   r e c o r d s
2   I work in a library. I _ _ _ _ _ _ _ _
3   A piece of hard paper or plastic. C _ _ _
4   Something flat to put books on. S _ _ _ _
5   Take for a short time and return it. B _ _ _ _ _
6   A list of all the books you can find in the library. C _ _ _ _ _ _ _ _

2 **Puzzle**
Complete the boxes with the words from exercise 1. You can use the
puzzle to help you.

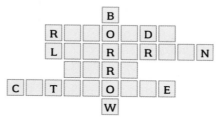

3 **The title**
Read about the title of the story. Why do you think the Tractate
Middoth is important in this story?

*The Tractate Middoth is a Jewish sacred text. This means the text has
religious importance. It is written in the language of Hebrew.*

A   It is an important sacred text.
B   The librarian only knows Hebrew.
C   There is some hidden information in the text.

The Visitor at the Library

t was late one Autumn afternoon. A man with a thin face and a large, curly moustache walked into a small but well-known university library. He put his card on the front desk. The librarian looked at the date on it.

'I understand that I can still use this library,' the man said.

'Of course, sir,' replied Mr Rogers, the librarian. 'I need to check,[1] but the card seems fine.'

The librarian looked at the records. The gentleman's name was Mr Eldred. The librarian could see that he didn't often use the library but he always returned his books on time. Mr Eldred waited.

'Do you think someone could find a book for me?' he asked impatiently. He gave the librarian a piece of paper with the title of the book.

1. **check** : look at something carefully to be sure.

Tractate Middoth

'It's in Hebrew,' he added.

At that moment a young student walked past. His name was William Garratt and he was working in the library to help pay for his studies. He was always cheerful[2] and a good worker.

'Mr Garratt,' called the older librarian. 'Could you please find a book for this gentleman?'

Mr Garratt said he was happy to help. He took the piece of paper and went towards the top floor of the library. Ten minutes later he returned without the book.

'I'm very sorry, sir,' he said. 'It's not on the shelf. I saw an old clergyman[3] with a book in his hand. I think he has that book. He's probably still in the library if you want to wait.'

'No, I can't stay,' Mr Eldred said quickly. 'I'm late for my train. I'll come back tomorrow.'

Mr Garratt did not have time to reply because Mr Eldred was already gone. The young man was sorry not to be able to help.

'Perhaps the old man wants to look at the book and doesn't need to take it home. I could ask him,' he thought.

He went back to the Hebrew section to see if he could find him. The book was on the shelf but the clergyman was not there.

Early the next morning Mr Eldred was at the library again. This time Mr Garratt saw him.

'I'm sorry you had to leave so early last night, sir,' he said. 'I returned to that section and the book was there. I'll go and get it for you straight away.'

Mr Eldred sat on a chair near the entrance and waited. He played with the ends of his moustache nervously.[4] He looked at

---

2. **cheerful** : happy and pleasant.
3. **clergyman** : a religious leader, for example, a priest.
4. **nervously** : in a worried way.

his watch often. Twenty minutes later he got up and went to the reception desk.

'Is it very far to that part of the library?' he asked angrily. 'Is that young man getting my book?'

'You're right,' said the librarian. 'Mr Garratt is usually very good but sometimes he does talk to his friends. These young students! I'll call that part of the library.'

The librarian picked up the telephone. He coughed and then he spoke in an important voice.

'Garratt, is that you?' he asked. 'Oh... I see. Alright. I'll let the gentleman know.'

'I'm very sorry,' the librarian said. 'Mr Garratt isn't feeling well. He had a sort of "attack".'[5]

The gentleman looked very worried. 'This attack...' said Mr Eldred in a low voice. 'Did someone attack him?'

'No. He wasn't attacked by a person,' replied the librarian. 'It was a nervous attack. He fainted. Please, don't go without your book, Mr Eldred. I can give you directions. You could find it yourself, if you prefer.'

'It won't be necessary,' said Mr Eldred suddenly. 'Can you send the book by post?'

'Let me see! Yes, we can send that book by post. There is a charge.'[6]

'That's not a problem, I'll return later with the money,' he said. He left immediately.

A few days later, a friend of William Garratt called George Earle came to visit. George also worked at the library. He was a friendly young man and often spoke with William at work.

'I'm not surprised you fainted,' he said. 'The air in that part of

---

5. **attack** : here, a sudden short illness.
6. **charge** : money for a service.

the library is terrible. And the dust is so thick. They should open the windows more often.'

'The air is bad,' agreed William. 'But that's not the reason why I fainted. George, this is going to sound strange, but I saw something.'

'You saw something,' George repeated. 'What did you see?'

His friend told his story.

'On Monday, a man came to the reception desk and asked about a book. The title was: 'Tractate Middoth'. It's in the Hebrew section. Maybe you know it; you're a theology student!'

'The Tractate Middoth is a Jewish sacred text,' said George.

'That's right,' continued William. 'Well, as you know, I went to find it. The book wasn't on the shelf but I saw a clergyman with a book in his hand. I returned to the desk to tell the gentleman, but he said he was very busy and he couldn't wait.

'On Tuesday, the man came to the library again. I went back to that section of the library to look for the book. There was a lot of dust in the air and the smell of something bad. I saw the same clergyman. He was standing next to the bookshelf. He was dressed in black. I could see the back of his head. He had very little hair. In fact, he had no hair at all. There were... cobwebs[7] on his head. I made a noise so he knew that someone was behind him. And then, he turned around and I saw his face...' William stopped for a moment.

'What's the matter, William? What did you see?' asked George.

'It's almost impossible to describe it,' he said. 'It wasn't a face. It was a skull[8] — a skeleton.[9] The eyes were deep and empty and from his eyebrows to the bottom of his teeth, there were cobwebs... thick, black, cobwebs!

7. **cobweb :**

8. **skull :** the bones in your head.
9. **skeleton :** all the bones in the body.

The text and **beyond**

1 Questions

Complete the sentences with a question word: who? what? when? where? Then answer the questions.

1 .... is the gentleman with the large grey curly moustache?
2 .... does he arrive at the beginning of the story?
3 .... goes to find the book for Mr Eldred?
4 .... does Mr Garratt see with a book?
5 .... does Mr Eldred say he will return?
6 .... is Mr Garratt when he faints?
7 .... does George Earle think his friend became ill?
8 .... does the clergyman have on his head and his face?

2 Characters

Read the sentences (1-5). Which person do they describe (A-E)? Match a person (A-E) to what they say (6-7).

A Mr Eldred	**C** Mr Earle	**E** the clergyman
B Mr Garratt	**D** the Librarian	

1 ☐ He was cheerful and helpful.
2 ☐ He had very little hair.
3 ☐ He spoke in an important voice.
4 ☐ He was impatient.
5 ☐ He was a theology student.

'He looked at his watch often.'

We can use words like *always, usually, often, sometimes* and *never* to describe how often we do something. These words usually go between the pronoun and the verb (but after the verb *to be*).

For example: 'I *always* listen to music'; 'I am *never* late'. *Often* and *sometimes* can also be at the beginning or the end of a sentence.

❸ Grammar

Complete the survey. Use the symbols to put ticks or a cross. Then write full sentences using the present simple.

Library Survey

How often do you use the library to do these things?

Always ✓✓✓✓   Often ✓✓✓   Sometimes ✓✓   Never ✗

1 Looking for information on the internet	
2 Reading books	
3 Going to the cafe	
4 Studying	
5 Borrowing books	

❹ KEY Joining the library

Read the information about the library. Fill in the information on the library membership form.

To become a member of the library you will need:

1 A letter with your name and address.
2 Identification: a driver's licence, a passport.
3 £2 for the card.

To: William.Jones@vwv.co.uk

Thank you for your enquiry about joining the library. You asked about identification. We don't need a driving licence. Your passport is fine.

Walton Community Library

First Name: [   ]

Surname: [   ]

Address: [3 King Steet, Walton   ]

identification: [   ]

£ ... [   ]

Before you read

1 **Vocabulary – Wills**

In the next chapter you will read about a 'will'. Choose the best description of a 'will'.

A ☐ A document that a person reads to all their relatives before they die before they sell the house.

B ☐ A document about the correct way to bury a person and to have a funeral.

C ☐ A document about what a person would like to happen to their money and their possessions when they die.

2 **Odd one out**

Look at the topics. Find the words you don't know. Which word is the odd one out?

Wills: lawyer, witness, signature, book

Funeral: burial, spider, coffin, church

Possessions: air, money, land, house

3 **Adjectives**

In the next chapter you will read the story of a lady called Mrs Simpson and her uncle, Dr Rant. Match the adjectives to their opposites. Can you guess who they describe, Mrs Simpson (S) or Dr Rant (R)?

		S	R
1	nice	☐	☐
2	greedy	☐	☐
3	rich	☐	☐
4	generous	☐	☐
5	ugly	☐	☐
6	poor	☐	☐
7	beautiful	☐	☐
8	nasty	☐	☐

The Will

illiam Garratt did not return to work straight away.[1] He took a short holiday by the sea. He needed the change of air. His destination was Burham-on-Sea. Burnham was a quiet town with some pretty houses and a nice beach. The train station was busy for the middle of the week. On the train a lot of the carriages[2] were full, but in one of the carriages there were some free seats. He entered and said 'hello' to the other passenger. The man did not reply. He was wearing a black coat and a black hat. His face was turned towards the window. Suddenly, he remembered the events

1. **straight away** : immediately.
2. **carriages** : here, part of train the passengers sit in.

in the library and he ran out of the carriage. He went straight into the next carriage, fell hard on the floor and fainted.

When he woke up a few moments later a kind lady was next to him. She spoke in a soft voice.

'Are you alright?' she asked. 'You fainted.'

She offered him something to drink.

Mr Garratt said he was feeling much better. He thanked the lady for her help. The lady was called Mrs Simpson and she was travelling with her daughter, Miss Emily Simpson. They were both very friendly and he soon forgot about the clergyman.

'Where are you going to stay in Burnham?' asked Mrs Simpson. 'Are you visiting relatives?'

'No,' Mr Garratt replied. 'It's just a holiday. I didn't have time to make a reservation. I hope it's not busy at this time of year. Do you know of any bed and breakfasts?'

Miss Simpson laughed shyly and Mr Garratt thought that she looked very pretty.

'We have a bed and breakfast,' said Mrs Simpson. 'We have a room free at the moment so you can always stay with us.'

During his stay, the ladies spoke to Mr Garratt often. One night, after dinner, they invited him to come and sit with them in their living room.

'We're friends now,' said Miss Simpson.

They spoke about many things that evening but mostly William Garratt and Emily Simpson talked about books.

'Well, I don't know much about books,' said Mrs Simpson. 'All I know is that there is one book that has never brought me any luck, [3] only sadness.'

---

3. **luck** : things that happen but are not planned, for example, to win money.

'I'm sorry to hear that,' said William. 'Books give me a lot of happiness. They give me a job, too!'

'I think we should explain about the book to Mr Garratt,' said Miss Simpson. 'Maybe he can help us.'

'Well, I don't want to trouble Mr Garratt with our private matters,'[4] replied Mrs Simpson. 'But, if he can help, I will happily tell him my story.'

'I had an on old uncle. His name was Dr Rant. He died about twenty years ago. He was quite well known in the area because he asked to be buried in a room underground.[5] He was dressed in his clergyman's clothes, sitting at a table. The room is in a field near his house. In the village, they say there is a ghost dressed as a clergyman, but I have never seen it.

'He wasn't a good clergyman. He held religious services at the church but he didn't help the poor or behave like a religious man. He had no family. He had one nephew, called John, and a niece — that's myself. I don't think he liked us very much. However, he promised to leave his money and the house to both of us when he died.

'One winter, he became very ill. I knew he didn't have long to live so I went to look after him. When I arrived at the house, I saw my cousin John. He was leaving in a horse and carriage and he was smiling.

My uncle was very weak. He slept a lot and he didn't talk much. One evening, he called me to his room.

'"Mary," he said. "There's a will. I'm going to give everything I own to your cousin, John."'

---

4. **matters** : subjects that a person needs to think or talk about.
5. **underground** : below the ground, in the earth.

'Well, I felt very upset. [6] I'm not a greedy person, Mr Garratt, but my husband and I weren't rich people. He told me this news with a very nasty smile on his face.

'"There's another thing," he added. "I don't like John so I've made a second will. In the second will, you keep everything. There's just one thing: I'm not going to tell you where it is! I'm going to give you the same information that I gave John. The will is in a book. It has signatures and a witness. John can find the book any time he wants, but I have thousands of books so he won't find it straight away. Also, not all my books are in this house. When I'm gone you'll find an envelope in my desk. This is your clue. And I'll tell you one more thing. Come closer, Mary. Listen to me! The book isn't in English. It's a pity [7] that you are probably too stupid to find it. It would be a nice house here for you and your husband.'

Then he laughed like a madman and started coughing violently. [8] I wanted to kill him with my own hands. But these were his last words. He died a few hours later.

Now, John has everything. He has the house, the land, the money. My husband died six years ago and I'm living here with Emily. We earn our money the best we can, but John Eldred has never answered any of my letters. He won't give me a penny of my uncle's money to help us.'

'Eldred?' said William. 'Did you say John Eldred? Is he a tall man about fifty years old, with a long, curly moustache?'

'Yes, that's right,' said Mrs Simpson. 'Why? Do you know him?'

6. **upset** : sad because someone makes you worried or angry.
7. **pity** : to feel sorry about something.
8. **violently** : here, very strongly.

'There was a man with the same name at the University library,' said William. 'He was asking about a book.'

'It's possible,' said Mrs Simpson. 'I think he has business at the University.'

'What about the envelope?' asked William. 'You said your uncle gave you an envelope. Do you still have it?'

Mrs Simpson went to a locked drawer and took out a small piece of paper.

'This was in the envelope,' she said. 'You can look at it if you want. I don't know what use it is!'

William looked carefully at the numbers and wrote them down.

The next morning, Mr Garratt left a note. He was sorry to leave early. He told them how much he enjoyed his stay and he hoped to see the ladies again soon. For now, there was an important piece of information he must find.

On his return, William Garratt thought about the book John Eldred was looking for. He could remember the books and their catalogue numbers. Why couldn't he remember this number? He looked at the thin, black lines of Dr Rant's writing. They reminded him of the lines of a cobweb. He quickly put the piece of paper in his pocket.

The text and **beyond**

1 **Comprehension check**

For each question choose the correct answer — A, B or C.

1 Why does Mr Garratt run out of the carriage?
  A ☐ There is nowhere to sit.
  B ☐ To talk to Mrs and Miss Simpson.
  C ☐ The man in the carriage looks like the clergyman.

2 Where does Mr Garratt stay in Burnham?
  A ☐ In Mrs Simpson's Bed and Breakfast.
  B ☐ In the hotel of Mrs Simpson's friend.
  C ☐ In the house of Dr Rant.

3 What is unusual about Dr Rant's burial?
  A ☐ He is buried in a room underground.
  B ☐ He is not buried in the village near his hall.
  C ☐ No-one knows where he is buried.

4 How many wills did Dr Rant make?
  A ☐ One.
  B ☐ Two.
  C ☐ None.

5 Who has the house, the land and the money?
  A ☐ Miss Simpson.
  B ☐ John Eldred.
  C ☐ Mrs Simpson's husband.

6 What is written on the paper in the envelope?
  A ☐ Mr Eldred's address.
  B ☐ A note for Mr Garratt.
  C ☐ Some numbers.

2 Summary

Put the sentences in the correct order to make a summary of Mrs Simpson's story about her uncle.

A ☐ He told her that the second will was in a book.

B ☐ One winter Mrs Simpson went to look after her uncle.

C ☐ He said there were two wills. The second will gave everything to her.

D ☐ He died after he told her about the will.

E ☐ He said he was going to give all his money and possessions to her cousin John.

F ☐ There was a clue to find the book in an envelope.

11 **3** **KEY** Listening – Places to stay

Listen to people describing where they prefer to stay when they go on holiday. Choose the best type of accommodation (1-4) for each person (A-D).

1 Self-catering   **3** Camping

2 Bed and Breakfast   **4** Hotel

A ....   **C** ....

B ....   **D** ....

4 Replying to a 'post'

Write a reply to the post. (A 'post' is a name for writing or photographs you put on the Internet for other people to see.)

This is the best holiday ever! All I need now is an ice-cream.

Possible answers: you could say where you are and say how it's different. You could say you would like to be on the beach, too. You decide!

68

Before you read

🔊12 **1** **KEY** Listening

Listen to the first part of Chapter One. For questions 1-4 put a tick under the correct answer.

1 What does the librarian send to Mr Eldred?

2 What time is it when Mr Garratt leaves the library?

3 How does Mr Garratt travel?

4 Mr Eldred's driver comes to the station. What does he take?

Bretfield Hall

Mr Garratt was in the library. He took out the small piece of paper in his pocket.

The library catalogue numbers had three parts. A book with the numbers 11334 could be found in section 1.13.34 or 11.33.4 for example. William looked at every section until he came to the last one — 11.3.34.

William felt a strange fear in his heart. As he came closer, the bad smell was there again. His mouth was dry and his body felt colder. He went towards the shelf — the book was not there. He ran downstairs to the front desk.

'Has someone taken this book out of the library?' he asked Mr Rogers, the librarian. He put the number in front of him.

'Do you think I remember all the numbers of the books that go out of this library?' replied Mr Rogers angrily.

'Alright, I'll ask another question. Has Mr Eldred come back to the library? Mr Eldred was the man with the long curly moustache. He came to ask about a book last week. I went to find it for him and then I went home sick. '

'Of course I remember him!' cried Mr Rogers. 'I wish all our visitors were like him. He was here yesterday. He gave me several pounds to post a book. It only cost a few pence so I accepted his kind gift [1] and wrote it in the book for gifts to the library. '

William went straight to the book and wrote down the address: Bretfield Hall, Burnham Lane.

'When did you send the parcel?' [2] asked William impatiently.

'The postman came for it around ten-thirty this morning,' said the librarian. He'll probably take it to the central office first. It'll be with Mr Eldred late this afternoon.'

There wasn't a moment to lose. It was one o'clock. He was able to catch the next train. It was a slow train and stopped at all the stations on the line. The same train also took the post to the villages on the way. Luckily, it was a small station and he soon found the station master's office. In the corner he saw a bag of parcels and letters.

'I'm waiting for a parcel for a gentleman called Mr Eldred,' he told the station master.

'You're too late, sir,' replied the station master. 'The driver of his carriage came for a parcel a few moments ago.'

'I must see him,' said Mr Garratt. 'Can you tell me the quickest way to Bretfield Hall?'

1. **gift** : a present; something you give (not sell) to someone.
2. **parcel** : object covered in paper to be sent in the post.

PART THREE

'If you're walking, you can go across the fields by the gate opposite the station,' said the station master. 'It's quicker than going along the road.'

Mr Garratt thanked the station master. He ran quickly across the fields. In the distance he could see a large house. 'That must be Bretfield Hall,' he thought.

He continued running until his legs felt weak. It was impossible; he could never travel as fast as the carriage. Suddenly, he heard the sound of horses. He was only a few metres in front of the carriage now. He thought of everything he could say but he knew Mr Eldred was not going to give him the book without asking questions.

Then he saw Mr Eldred getting out of the carriage. One of the horses did not want to continue. The driver was shouting at the horse and Mr Eldred was shouting at the driver. Mr Garratt hid behind a tree. Mr Eldred went into the field and started walking towards the house. He took off the paper from the parcel. William followed him carefully. Finally Mr Eldred stopped under a tree. He opened the book and started to tear a page from it. At that moment a dark leaf fell to the ground. Mr Eldred jumped. A black cloud of a thousand tiny insects came from the tree. They covered[3] Mr Eldred's face and his neck. He kicked his arms and legs violently but no sound came from his mouth. Moments later, Mr Eldred was lying on the grass. Mr Garratt came closer. Mr Eldred was dead.

'Help!' he cried. 'This man needs a doctor!' The carriage was gone. A farmer in the next field came towards him.

'I think we should call the police,' he said. 'This man is dead.'

---

3. **covered** : went over it so you it was not possible to see.

PART THREE

The police took the book. William wanted to explain the importance of the book to the police. He hoped they believed him. Finally, they called Mr Garratt to explain why he was in the area at the time of Mr Eldred's death. Mr Garratt told them his story.

'There was no-one near the tree,' he said. 'There was a cloud of black dust at the same time Mr Eldred fell to the ground. I couldn't do anything. I called for help immediately.'

'There was some black dust on his lips,' said the sergeant. 'We can't find a reason for it. Perhaps it was earth. We don't think you murdered[4] him, Mr Garratt. Mr Eldred died of a heart attack. The question is: why did he die so suddenly?'

'I think it was the book,' said Mr Garratt. 'Mr Eldred was tearing a page from the book.'

The sergeant looked at Mr Garratt for a moment.

'Mr Garratt, you have come a long way for this book. Why is this book so important to you?'

Mr Garratt explained about the will. He told them about Mrs Simpson and Dr Rant, her uncle, and everything he could remember.

'Dr Rant was a clergyman at St Thomas. Are you saying Dr Rant wrote the will in the book?' asked one of the police officers.

'It's not good to speak about the dead, but there aren't many people that liked him in the village. If Mr Garratt is telling the truth then the shock[5] of seeing the will could kill a man with a weak heart.

'Johnson, call a lawyer!' he said to a police officer.

4. **murdered** : killed.
5. **shock** : a big surprise; it can make someone feel ill.

'We will need someone who can read Hebrew to read this,' said Inspector Johnson.

'No, we won't,' said the older man. 'The book is in Hebrew but this page is in English.'

He pointed to the torn page.

The lawyer arrived a few hours later. He looked at the torn page. There were three names: Dr Rant, the name of a lawyer and a witness. On the page there were also three signatures and the date.

The lawyer read the text. 'I give all my possessions, including the house and my land to Mrs Mary Simpson of Burnham-on-Sea'. He looked carefully at the signatures.

'It's a legal will,' he said. 'Dr Rant's belongings must go to his niece, Mrs Simpson.'

Mr Garratt was very happy. He went to tell Mrs Simpson the news.

Mr Garratt returned to the area quite often that year, and in the summer he went back to Bretfield. He and Miss Emily Simpson were happily married and they lived in the hall with its new owner,[6] Mrs Simpson.

Once, on the way home, Mr Garratt stopped at a tree. On the grass, in the leaves, he saw an ugly knot of cobwebs. He picked up a stick and touched it. Something moved quickly and then, from the cobweb, several large spiders climbed across his foot and ran into the leaves. He never saw them again.

---

6. **owner** : the person it belongs to.

The text and **beyond**

1 **KEY** Comprehension check

Are the sentences Right (A) or Wrong (B)? If there is not enough information to answer A or B, choose 'Doesn't say' (C).

1 The book Mr Garratt was looking for was in the library.
   A ☐ Right   B ☐ Wrong   C ☐ Doesn't say

2 Mr Eldred paid three pounds to send the book.
   A ☐ Right   B ☐ Wrong   C ☐ Doesn't say

3 The train to Bretfield was a fast train.
   A ☐ Right   B ☐ Wrong   C ☐ Doesn't say

4 Mr Garratt went across the fields to get to Bretfield Hall.
   A ☐ Right   B ☐ Wrong   C ☐ Doesn't say

5 The carriage stopped because the wheel broke.
   A ☐ Right   B ☐ Wrong   C ☐ Doesn't say

6 The policeman said Mr Eldred died of a heart attack.
   A ☐ Right   B ☐ Wrong   C ☐ Doesn't say

7 William Garratt married Emily Simpson in July.
   A ☐ Right   B ☐ Wrong   C ☐ Doesn't say

13 **2** **KEY** Listening – At the post office

You will hear a woman asking about sending a parcel at the post office. Complete the information.

POST OFFICE	
By:	airmail
Destination (country):	
Weight: 1/2 a	
Cost: £	
Contents:	and shoes

3 Speaking – Giving directions

Draw a map. Mark three places on the map. The place can be real or imaginary, for example, a school or hidden treasure. With a partner, ask questions about how to get to the places on the map.

4 Spooky Corner

What scares you?

A Write about a time you were scared using the questions and the examples to help you.

1 When was it? *About three years ago.*

2 Where was it? *I was on holiday.*

3 Who or what was it? *I saw a big spider.*

4 What happened? *It fell from a tree.*

5 How did you feel? *I felt/I was... frightened/terrified/afraid.*

6 What did you do? *I ran away/I screamed/I jumped.*

B Do ghosts or imaginary creatures scare you?

Ghosts and monsters

Match a word to the pictures below. Do you know of any other imaginary creatures?

A ghost   **B** zombie   **C** vampire

The Woman in Black

Title : The Woman in Black
Date : 2012
Director : James Watkins
Actor : Daniel Radcliffe as Arthur Kipps

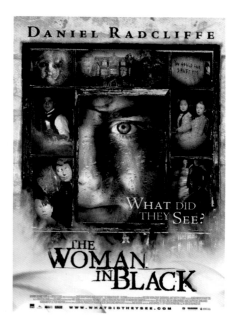

Mr Arthur Kipps, remembers the story of a house he once visited and the terrifying events that happened there. This is when the story begins. Arthur Kipps is a young lawyer. Eel Marsh House stands in a lonely place. It is only possible to reach it when the sea is low. Arthur attends the funeral of the lady who lived in the house, called Alice. At the funeral he sees a young woman dressed in black. The people in the village know about the lady, but they won't talk about her or the secret of Eel Marsh House. But Arthur will soon find out when he spends the night at the house.

A brilliant film with lots of scary moments.

1 **Read the review of the film *The Woman in Black*. Write your own review of a scary film. Example:**

This film is very good. There is a ghost and the ghost has a sad story. The man helps her. I liked the ending. It was very scary.

① The characters

Who is this? Match each sentence (1-10) to a character (A-J) from one of the stories.

A ☐ The Colonel	**F** ☐	Mr Brown
B ☐ Mr Disney	**G** ☐	Mr Eldred
C ☐ Dr Rant	**H** ☐	Mrs Simpson
D ☐ Professor Parkins	**I** ☐	Mr Garratt
E ☐ Mr Somerton	**J** ☐	Mr Gregory

1 He was intelligent and shy.
He didn't believe in ghosts.

2 He was loud and had red cheeks.
He played golf with the professor.

3 She was helpful and friendly.
She became very rich.

4 He was nasty and greedy.
He wrote two wills.

5 He was clever and greedy.
He wanted to find a bag of gold.

6 He was kind.
He went to help his friend in Steinfield.

7 He had a moustache and he was impatient.
He was looking for a book.

8 He was helpful and cheerful.
He married Miss Simpson.

9 He was a good servant.
He helped his master from the well.

10 He was curious and asked a lot of questions.
He was interested in the ruins.

This reader uses the **EXPANSIVE READING** approach, where the text becomes a springboard to improve language skills and to explore historical background, cultural connections and other topics suggested by the text.

The new structures introduced in this step of our **READING & TRAINING** series are listed below. Naturally, structures from lower steps are included too. For a complete list of structures used over all the six steps, see *The Black Cat Guide to Graded Readers*, which is also downloadable at no cost from our website, blackcat-cideb.com.

The vocabulary used at each step is carefully checked against vocabulary lists used for internationally recognised examinations.

Step **One** **A2**

All the structures used in the previous levels, plus the following:

Verb tenses
Present Simple
Present Continuous
Past Simple
Past Continuous
Future reference: Present Continuous; *going to*; *will*; Present Simple
Present Perfecst Simple: indefinite past with *ever, never* (for experience)

Verb forms and patterns
Regular and common irregular verbs
Affirmative, negative, interrogative
Imperative: 2nd person; *let's*
Passive forms: Present Simple; Past Simple
Short answers
Infinitives after verbs and adjectives
Gerunds (verb + *-ing*) after prepositions and common verbs
Gerunds (verb + *-ing*) as subjects and objects

Modal verbs
Can: ability; requests; permission
Could: ability; requests
Will: future reference; offers; promises; predictions
Would … like: offers, requests
Shall: suggestions; offers
Should (present and future reference): advice

May (present and future reference): possibility
Must: personal obligation
Mustn't: prohibition
Have (got) to: external obligation
Need: necessity

Types of clause
Co-ordination: *but; and; or; and then*
Subordination (in the Present Simple or Present Continuous) after verbs such as: *to be sure; to know; to think; to believe; to hope; to say; to tell*
Subordination after: *because, when, if* (zero and 1st conditionals)
Defining relative clauses with: *who, which, that*, zero pronoun, *where*

Other
Zero, definite and indefinite articles
Possessive *'s* and *s'*
Countable and uncountable nouns
Some, any; much, many, a lot; (a) little, (a) few; all, every; etc.
Order of adjectives
Comparative and superlative of adjectives (regular and irregular)
Formation and comparative/ superlative of adverbs (regular and irregular)